Awesome Bugs

BEES

and

WASPS

Anna Claybourne

FRANKLIN WATTS
London • Sydney

Produced by:
Aladdin Books Ltd
28 Percy Street
London W1T 2BZ

ISBN 0–7496–5491–0

*First published in
Great Britain in 2004 by:*
Franklin Watts
96 Leonard Street
London
EC2A 4XD

Editor:
Harriet Brown

Designer:
Flick, Book Design & Graphics

Illustrators:
Aziz Khan, Tony Swift,
Norman Weaver
Cartoons: Jo Moore

Certain illustrations have
appeared in earlier books
created by Aladdin Books.

Printed in UAE

Contents

Introduction

Bees and wasps are everywhere. Not just plain old honeybees and common wasps, but all their awesome relatives too – from tiny gall wasps to giant wood wasps, big furry bumblebees and massive tarantula hawk wasps that feed on huge, hairy spiders. In this book, you can find out what bees and wasps eat, why they sting and how they communicate with each other. Why do bees make wax and honey, while wasps make paper and ink? If you're ready to step into the world of these amazing insects, read on...

Spot and count, and more fun facts!

Q: Why watch out for these boxes?

A: They answer the bee and wasp questions you always wanted to ask.

zoom in on...

Bits and pieces

Look out for these boxes to take a closer look at bee and wasp features.

Awesome facts
Watch out for these diamonds to learn more about the truly weird and wonderful world of bees and wasps.

What are bees and wasps?

Bees and wasps are insects, and like all insects, they have six legs and two antennae (feelers). They also have four wings, and most of them can fly and sting. But there are differences between them too. Bees are hairier, and feed mainly on flowers. Wasps often have brighter colours, and they hunt other animals.

Q: Why do bees and wasps buzz?

A: The buzzing you can hear when a bee or wasp flies past is made by its wings flapping very fast – up to 200 times a second! The buzz warns other animals, including humans, that a bee or wasp is nearby, and that they should leave it alone if they don't want to get stung. Some bees and wasps also use their wings as fans to cool down their nests. That's why a wasps' nest or a beehive often makes a loud buzzing sound.

Body parts

Here's a closer look at a typical bee – a honeybee – and a typical wasp – a common paper wasp.

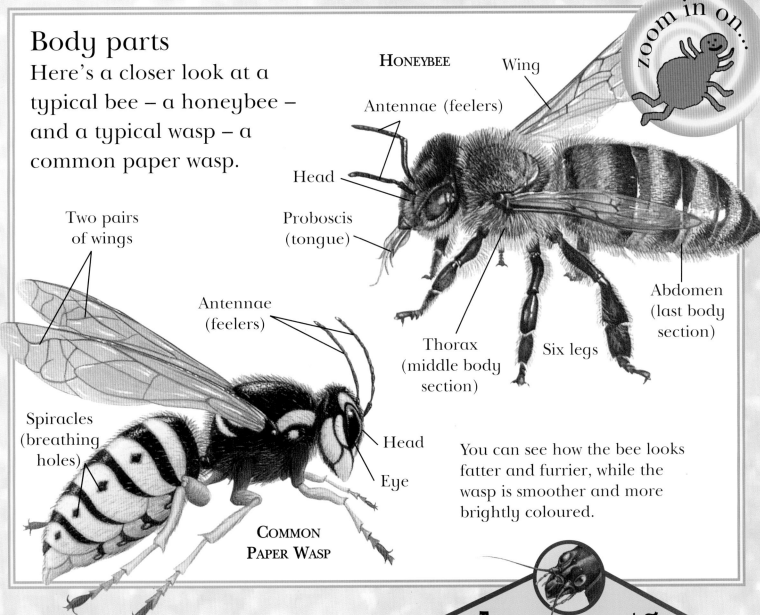

HONEYBEE

Wing

Antennae (feelers)

Head

Proboscis (tongue)

Thorax (middle body section)

Six legs

Abdomen (last body section)

Two pairs of wings

Antennae (feelers)

Spiracles (breathing holes)

Head

Eye

COMMON PAPER WASP

You can see how the bee looks fatter and furrier, while the wasp is smoother and more brightly coloured.

Different types of bees and wasps live in almost every part of the world. The only places they don't live are the frozen areas around the Poles, and the tops of high mountains, where it's too cold and windy for them. Many bees and wasps, including honeybees, are social insects. They live together in groups, called colonies.

Awesome facts

There are around 20,000 species (types) of bees. No one really knows how many wasp species there are, but it's probably more than 100,000!

Bees and wasps are good at seeing fast movements, but not slow ones.

Honeybees can see a kind of light that humans can't, called ultraviolet. But they can't see red – it looks black to them.

In this close-up picture of a bee's face, you can see the two big compound eyes on the sides of its head. Compound eyes are actually made up of thousands of tiny eyes joined together. In between the two compound eyes, a bee or wasp has three smaller, simpler eyes, called ocelli. So bees and wasps have five eyes altogether!

Sensational senses

Just like us, bees and wasps use their senses to help them find their way around, detect food and communicate with each other. Sight and smell are probably their most important senses. Most bees and wasps have huge eyes called compound eyes, which take up most of their heads. Instead of having noses, they use their antennae to smell things.

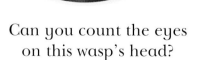

Can you count the eyes on this wasp's head?

6 The antennae are used to taste and feel things, too.

Antenna

Bees' and wasps' antennae are made up of a row of sections, called segments, joined together.

Q: Do bees and wasps have ears?

A: They don't have ears like humans do, but they can still sense some sounds. This is because sounds make vibrations in the air. Bees and wasps can detect these vibrations with their skin, legs or antennae.

The ichneumon wasp below has unusually long antennae.

Three ocelli (simple eyes)

Compound eye

This diagram shows some of the sense organs on a wasp's head.

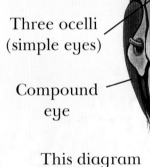

Compound eye

Honeybees are good at seeing blue and purple colours, and they are often attracted to blue and purple flowers. Some flowers have lines on them that lead to the middle of the flower. Scientists think these lines, called 'honeyguides', help bees to find and feed on flower nectar.

7

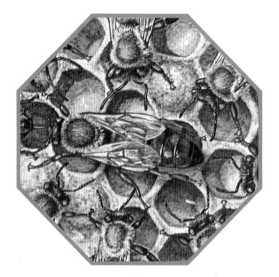

Sending messages

Many types of bees and wasps live together in large colonies, so they have to be able to give each other messages and instructions. But they don't talk in words like we do. Instead, bees and wasps mainly communicate using smells called pheromones. Honeybees also do special dances to tell each other where to find the best flowers.

Most bee and wasp colonies have a leader called the queen. She constantly releases a pheromone scent to let the other bees or wasps know she is safe. If they don't sense the pheromone, they know the queen must be missing.

Awesome facts

When a wasp gets squashed, its body releases a special scent that tells other wasps to be on the lookout for danger.

When bees or wasps are all together inside their nest or hive, it's usually too dark to see. Instead, they feel and smell each other using their antennae. Using smells to send messages is very effective because they spread quickly through the nest.

zoom in on...

Dancing bees

When a honeybee finds a good patch of flowers to feed on, she goes back to the nest or hive to tell the other bees about it. To do this, bees do special dances that explain how far away the flowers are, and what direction to fly in to find them. The other bees follow and touch the dancing bee to find out what she is saying.

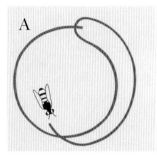

Dance (A) is called the round dance. It's used to describe food that's nearby – up to 30 m away. The other bees can smell the scent of the flowers on the bee, and this helps them to track the flowers down.

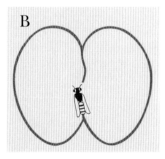

Dance (B) is called the waggle dance. It means the food is over 30 m away. The bee dances a figure-of-eight pattern and wags her tail. The middle part of the dance shows the direction of the food in relation to the Sun.

This dance says the food is opposite the Sun.

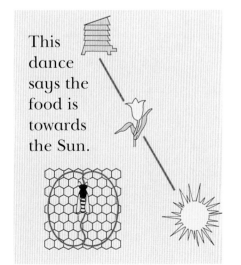

This dance says the food is towards the Sun.

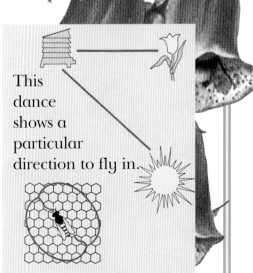

This dance shows a particular direction to fly in.

Q: Where does beeswax come from?

A: Beeswax is a thick, greasy wax that a bee makes inside its body. The wax is squeezed out of the bee's body between special scales on its stomach. From there, the bee collects the wax with its feet, and chews it in its jaws, before adding it to the walls of the nest.

Home sweet home – bees

Bees that live in groups make themselves a nest to live in. Wild honeybees use wax to build a dangling nest attached to a tree. Domestic honeybees live in artificial hives (see page 28). Other social bees make different types of nests – bumblebees, for example, live in a hole in the ground, lined with grass or moss.

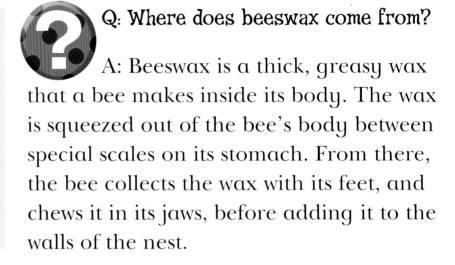

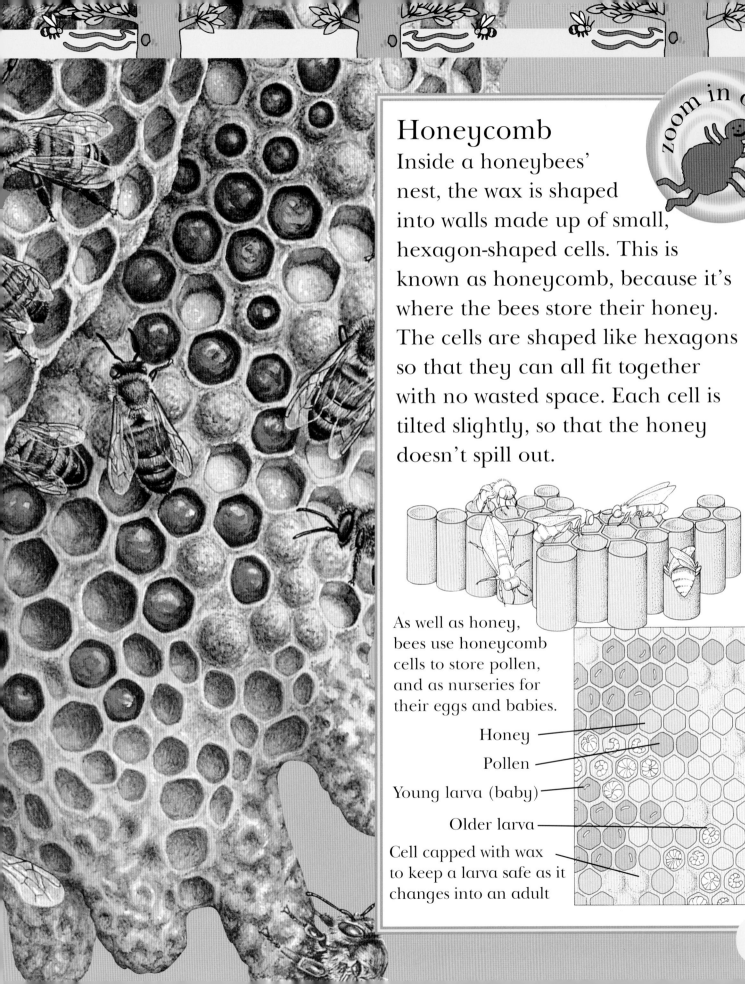

Honeycomb

Inside a honeybees' nest, the wax is shaped into walls made up of small, hexagon-shaped cells. This is known as honeycomb, because it's where the bees store their honey. The cells are shaped like hexagons so that they can all fit together with no wasted space. Each cell is tilted slightly, so that the honey doesn't spill out.

As well as honey, bees use honeycomb cells to store pollen, and as nurseries for their eggs and babies.

Honey

Pollen

Young larva (baby)

Older larva

Cell capped with wax to keep a larva safe as it changes into an adult

11

zoom in on...

Nest building

Paper wasps' nests are round or oval. Inside, the wasps build several layers of cells. They build the layers at the top first, and then add more layers underneath. The layers are connected by strands of wasp paper.

These yellow jackets are a type of social wasp. They usually build round nests.

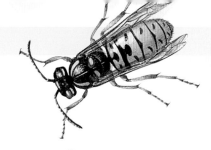

Wasps' nests

Common wasps build their nests out of paper. They scrape wood from fence posts or dead trees and mix it with saliva (spit) to make a papery pulp. This is why they're also known as paper wasps. Like bees, they give their nest smooth outer walls, and build hexagonal cells inside for raising their young.

A queen wasp starting to build an underground nest

If you ever see a wasps' nest, leave it alone! Wasps can get annoyed if their nest is disturbed.

Common wasps build their nests underground in an abandoned animal burrow, or in an empty space such as a loft or an old garden shed. Each colony is started by a queen, who finds a good place to nest and starts laying eggs there. When the first babies have become adults, they help the queen to build the whole nest.

Drone bee

Worker bee

Queen bee

Colonies and queens

A colony is the name for a group of social bees or wasps that all live together. They all help to find food, build a nest, bring up babies and fight off enemies. In a colony, different bees and wasps have different jobs to do. There are lots of workers, a few drones, and the queen, who lays eggs and controls the colony.

A worker feeding a larva (baby) inside a cell

A worker feeding another, newly-hatched worker

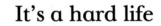

It's a hard life

Worker bees and wasps are all female. They do all kinds of everyday jobs for the colony, including collecting food, feeding babies, making wax, honey or paper, building cells and cleaning the nest. However, they can't lay eggs themselves.

A new adult worker emerging from her cell

small for them to feed on their own.

Drones

A drone is one of the male bees or wasps in a colony. Drones are usually slightly bigger than workers. Their job is to mate with the queen, so that she can lay eggs. When this is done, the workers sometimes throw the drones out.

zoom in on...

Worker bees pushing an old drone out of their nest

Q: Why live in a colony?

A: Living in a group is a good way to stay safe and find enough food, as all the workers in a colony help and protect each other. In fact, some scientists say that a colony acts almost like a single animal, made up of many separate parts.

This is a new honeybee queen hatching out of her cell. The cell has an unusual, extra-long shape.

The queen

Although workers are female, they don't usually lay eggs. This job is done by the queen, a special female. She also controls the colony using pheromone smells (see page 8). If an old honeybee queen dies or leaves the nest, the workers can make new queens by feeding them special food. Sometimes, new queens fight to become the colony leader.

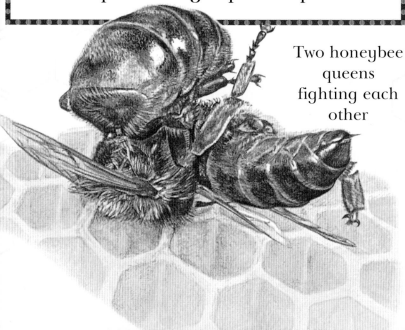

Two honeybee queens fighting each other

15

Bringing up babies

Like most insects, bees and wasps have babies by laying eggs. The eggs hatch out into little worm-like babies called larvae. These grow bigger and bigger, before finally changing into adults. In a colony of social bees or wasps, the workers all help to feed and care for the babies inside the nest.

The big picture on these two pages shows paper wasps caring for their larvae.

These two worker honeybees are busy feeding larvae inside their nest. You can see two white, curled-up larvae inside the cells. One of the bees is reaching into another cell to feed another larva with food using her mouth.

The larvae in this picture are quite large. Soon, the workers will cover their cells with wax caps. Inside, they will turn into adults, then climb out.

Awesome facts

A honeybee queen can lay nearly 2,000 eggs a day. In her whole lifetime, she can have over a million babies!

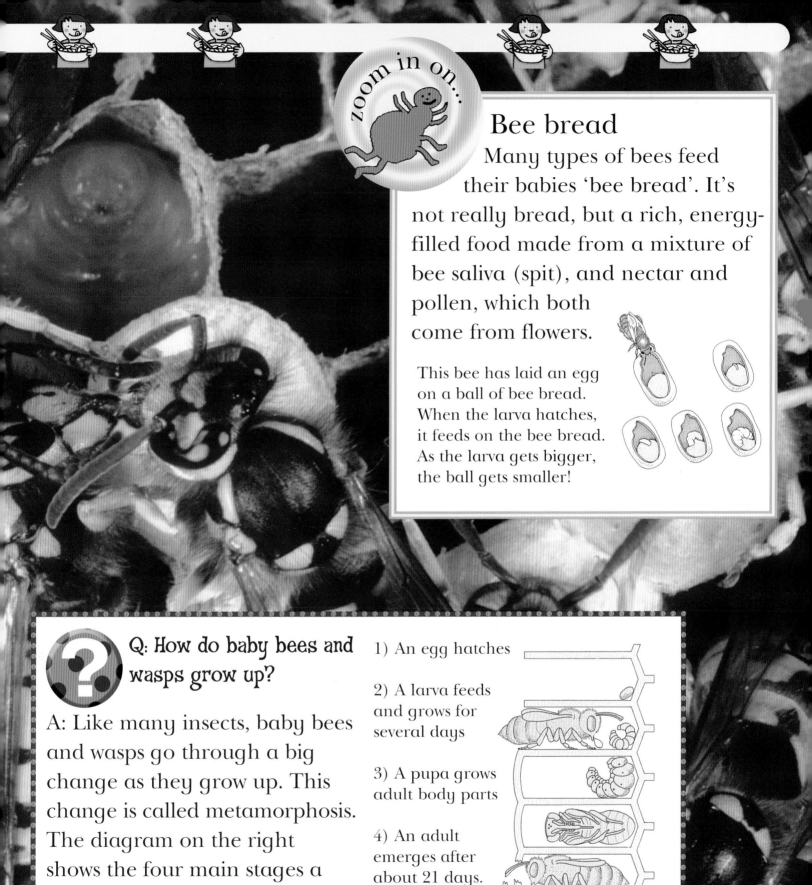

Bee bread

Many types of bees feed their babies 'bee bread'. It's not really bread, but a rich, energy-filled food made from a mixture of bee saliva (spit), and nectar and pollen, which both come from flowers.

This bee has laid an egg on a ball of bee bread. When the larva hatches, it feeds on the bee bread. As the larva gets bigger, the ball gets smaller!

Q: How do baby bees and wasps grow up?

A: Like many insects, baby bees and wasps go through a big change as they grow up. This change is called metamorphosis. The diagram on the right shows the four main stages a honeybee goes through.

1) An egg hatches

2) A larva feeds and grows for several days

3) A pupa grows adult body parts

4) An adult emerges after about 21 days.

Egg

Food ball

CARPENTER BEE

Carpenter bee

Carpenter bees burrow into wood, either in dead trees, or in buildings, fences or telegraph poles. They make a series of chambers and leave an egg in each one, along with a ball of pollen and nectar for the baby to feed on when it hatches.

zoom in on...

Ichneumon wasps

Ichneumon wasps aren't true wasps, but are closely related to them. They appear to have a huge sting, but it's really just an ovipositor – a special tube for laying eggs deep inside wood.

An ichneumon wasp drills into a tree trunk to lay an egg on the larva (young) of another insect. When the young wasp hatches, it will feed on the larva.

A potter wasp stuffing a caterpillar into a pot to feed her young

Potter wasp

Potter wasps make tiny pot-shaped nests out of mud. The adult wasp catches a caterpillar or other baby insect, stings it and stuffs it into the pot. Then she lays an egg inside the pot, and seals the top. When the baby hatches, it feeds on the caterpillar.

18

Living alone

Instead of living in colonies, some bees and wasps live on their own. They are known as solitary bees and wasps. Each individual finds its own food, makes its own nests and cares for its own babies. Solitary bees and wasps include carpenter bees, leafcutter bees, mason wasps, hawk wasps and ichneumon wasps.

This mother mason wasp is building a long tube out of mud. The tube protects the entrance to the burrow where she shelters her young.

Leafcutter bees

You can tell when a leafcutter bee has been at work by the neat semicircle-shaped holes cut out of leaves. The bee uses the leaf pieces to make cells to lay her eggs in. She stacks the cells, each containing an egg and a food supply, inside her nest. This can be a hole in some rotten wood, the inside of a plant stem, or sometimes an old snail shell.

Look out for leaves cut by leafcutter bees, potter wasps' pots, and carpenter bee holes in parks and gardens near your home.

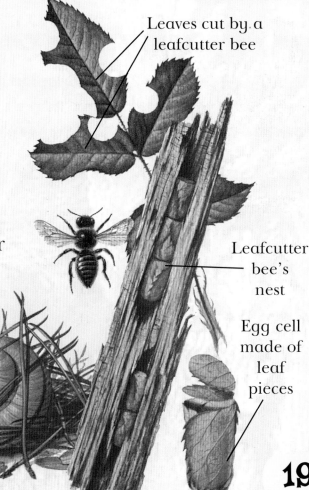

Leaves cut by a leafcutter bee

Leafcutter bee's nest

Egg cell made of leaf pieces

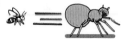

Face and jaws of a
common wasp

What do wasps eat?

Most wasps are fierce hunters. They use their stings to kill or paralyse other animals – usually spiders, other insects, or insect larvae such as fat, juicy caterpillars. However, this food is usually not for the adult wasp, but for its young. Adult wasps themselves are omnivores. This means they'll eat all kinds of food, including flowers, fruit and meat.

 Q: Why do wasps buzz around our food?

A: Wasps like sweet drinks, cakes, fruit and other sugary food, because it gives them the energy they need for flying around. They often find what they're looking for at our picnics, in shop windows or in dustbins.

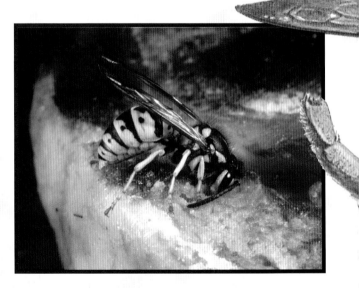

Wasps have strong jaws called mandibles, which they use for eating and sometimes for killing their prey, too. The mandibles slice together like a pair of scissors to chew up all kinds of food, even tough food like raw meat.

much bigger than itself.

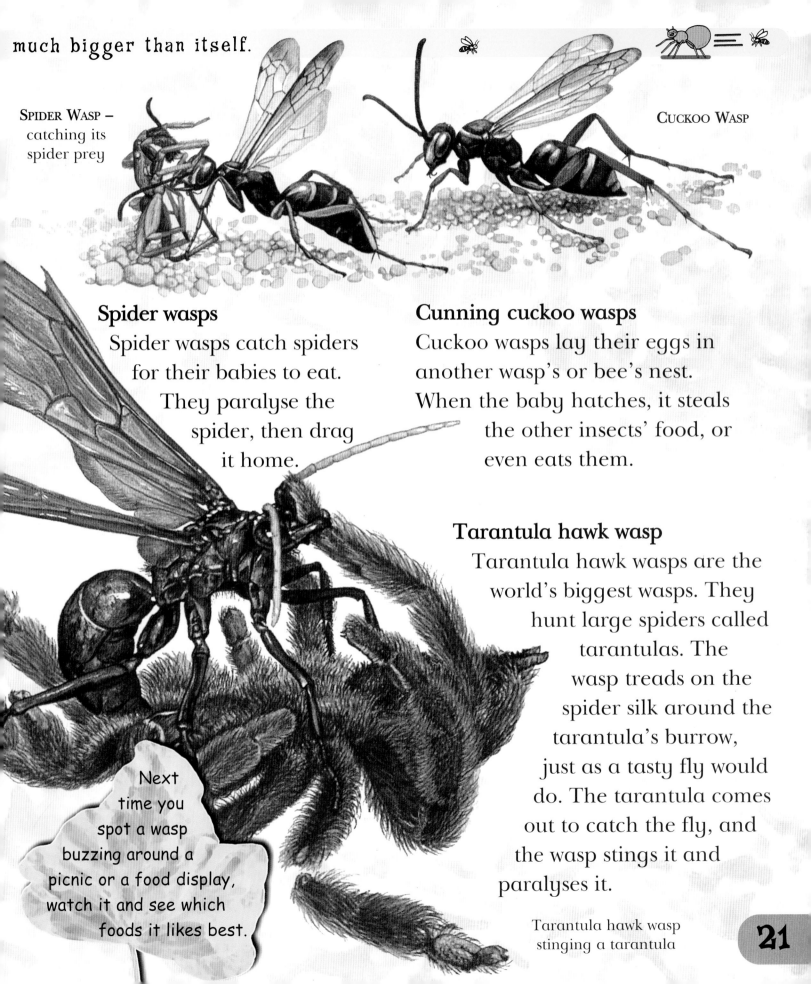

SPIDER WASP – catching its spider prey

CUCKOO WASP

Spider wasps

Spider wasps catch spiders for their babies to eat. They paralyse the spider, then drag it home.

Cunning cuckoo wasps

Cuckoo wasps lay their eggs in another wasp's or bee's nest. When the baby hatches, it steals the other insects' food, or even eats them.

Tarantula hawk wasp

Tarantula hawk wasps are the world's biggest wasps. They hunt large spiders called tarantulas. The wasp treads on the spider silk around the tarantula's burrow, just as a tasty fly would do. The tarantula comes out to catch the fly, and the wasp stings it and paralyses it.

Next time you spot a wasp buzzing around a picnic or a food display, watch it and see which foods it likes best.

Tarantula hawk wasp stinging a tarantula

Q: Do bees drink?

A: Yes! Like most animals, they need to drink water to stay healthy and keep them from drying out. Bees usually sip water from small puddles, or visit ponds that have leaves or pebbles in them to land on. Bees suck water up using their tube-like tongues.

What do bees eat?

Bees are vegetarians. They feed on nectar and pollen from flowers, and on honey, which they make from nectar. But bees don't just go out and find food for themselves. Like wasps, they collect food and bring it home to their nests to feed their babies. In colonies, worker bees also collect food for other bees, such as the queen and the drones. They store food in their nests to eat in winter, too.

zoom in on...

What are nectar and pollen?

Nectar and pollen are a bee's favourite foods. Nectar is a sweet, sugary juice found deep inside flowers. Bees suck nectar into their stomachs using their tongues, then make it into honey when they get back to their nest. Pollen is a yellow dust found in flowers. Bees carry it by rolling it into balls, which they fasten to their knees (below).

To make seeds, flowers have to exchange some pollen with each other. As bees collect nectar and pollen, they help flowers by spreading a few specks of pollen from one flower to the next. This is called pollination.

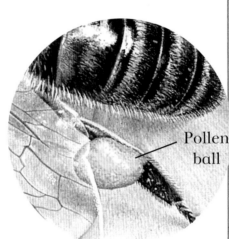

Pollen ball

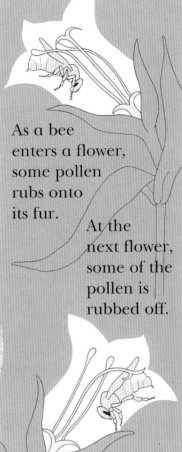

As a bee enters a flower, some pollen rubs onto its fur.

At the next flower, some of the pollen is rubbed off.

Awesome facts

In a single day, a worker honeybee can fly up to 80 km and visit over 2,000 different flowers.

The bumblebee year

Every autumn, when it gets cold, most of the bees in a bumblebee colony die. Only young queen bumblebees survive. They spend the winter alone, hibernating (sleeping) somewhere safe and dry. In spring, each queen starts a new colony.

In winter, a bumblebee queen hibernates under a pile of leaves, or in a hole in the ground lined with dead grass.

zoom in on...

Wax garlands

When honeybees need to build a new honeycomb, they cling together in long, hanging chains, called wax garlands. As the bees hang from each other, their bodies start to produce lots of wax, which they use to build new cells and nest walls.

Wax garland

By midsummer, the queen has found a place to nest, and has laid lots of eggs which have hatched into new workers. New queens are born in late summer.

24

Through the year

In places that have a cold winter, it's hard for insects to survive all year round. Some bees and wasps get through the cold season by huddling together inside their nests and eating stored food such as honey. In other species, most of the bees or wasps die in the autumn, leaving just a few young queens alive. The queens, who have fertilised eggs inside them, hibernate through the winter, and start new colonies in the spring.

Q: Why do bees swarm?

A: Sometimes a honeybee colony grows too big for its nest or hive. When this happens, the queen leaves, taking about half of the bees with her, to build a new nest somewhere else. This swarm can contain over 20,000 bees – but they are just looking for a new home, not trying to chase people. The remaining bees raise a new queen.

Stinging and safety

Bees and wasps are famous for stinging. Wasps use their stings to kill and paralyse their prey. Bees and wasps also use their stings to defend themselves. A painful sting is very useful for putting off an attacker, even one that's many times bigger than a tiny insect.

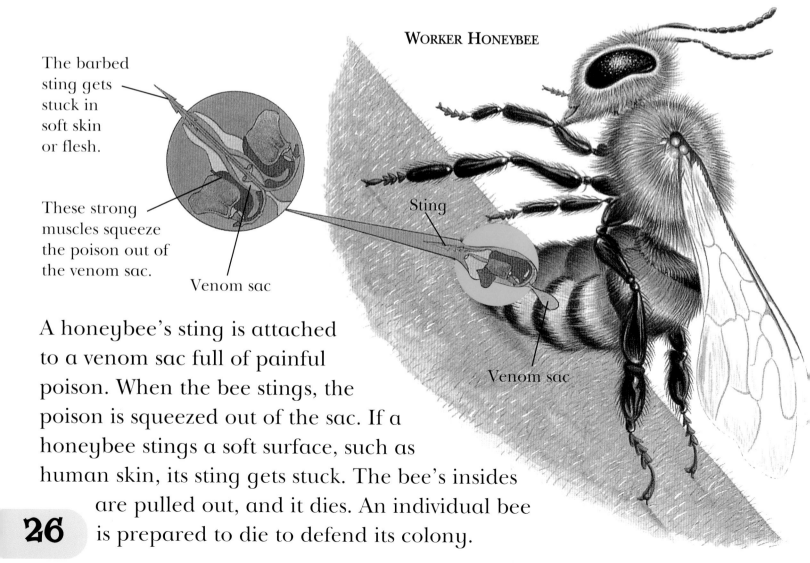

WORKER HONEYBEE

The barbed sting gets stuck in soft skin or flesh.

These strong muscles squeeze the poison out of the venom sac.

Venom sac

Sting

Venom sac

A honeybee's sting is attached to a venom sac full of painful poison. When the bee stings, the poison is squeezed out of the sac. If a honeybee stings a soft surface, such as human skin, its sting gets stuck. The bee's insides are pulled out, and it dies. An individual bee is prepared to die to defend its colony.

Only the females have stings.

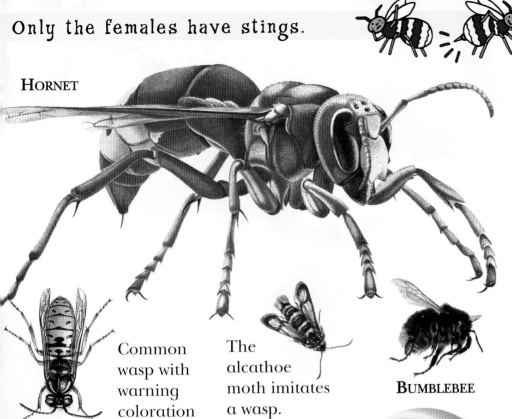

HORNET

Common wasp with warning coloration

The alcathoe moth imitates a wasp.

BUMBLEBEE

A few people are allergic to bee or wasp stings. For them, a sting can be deadly, unless they get the right medicine fast.

Most bee and wasp stings are painful, but not dangerous. Beekeepers get stung all the time, with no ill effects. Some people believe the stings of hornets, a type of large wasp, are the most serious, but in fact they are very similar to other bee and wasp stings. Being stung can even relieve some illnesses, such as rheumatism.

Warning signs

Stinging insects often have bright stripes or spots, especially in orange, yellow or black, to warn other animals of the danger. This is called warning coloration, and many bees and wasps have it. Some other insects, including harmless beetles, moths and flies, mimic (copy) bees' and wasps' markings, to make predators think they can sting, too.

Hoverflies can often be mistaken for wasps.

The bee hawk moth resembles a bee.

zoom in on...

Killer bees

Killer bees are a type of honeybee. They were taken from Africa to South America in an attempt to breed bees that could live in a hot climate. But instead, the bee breeders ended up with aggressive bees that sometimes chase and sting people for no reason. However, some movies have exaggerated the numbers and killer instincts of these bees.

How do bees make honey?

When a bee gets to the hive with a load of nectar, she passes it to another bee. In this bee's body, special chemicals called enzymes are added to the nectar. Then the bee puts the nectar in a cell. The bees fan the nectar to dry it out, and it slowly turns into thick honey.

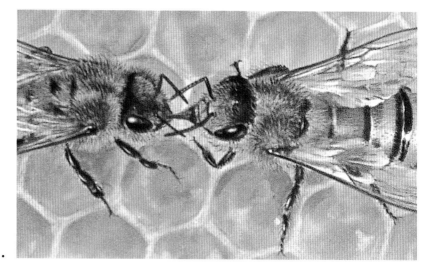

Beekeeping

Beekeepers give bees artificial homes, called hives, to live in. They also give them extra food to replace the honey they take away. A modern beehive looks like a tiny house. It contains lots of wooden frames where the bees can build their wax honeycomb. It also has an entrance for the bees to fly in and out, and a removeable lid so that the beekeeper can reach the honey.

zoom in on...

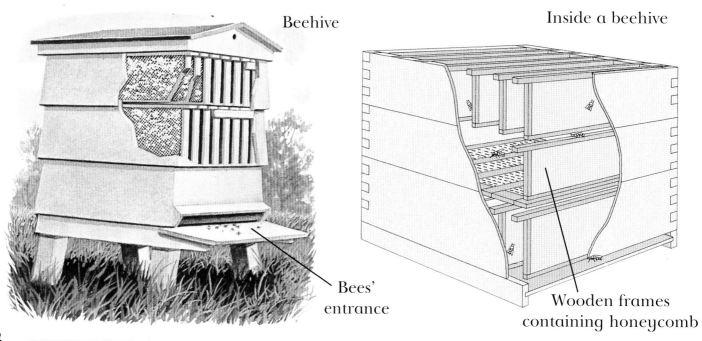

Beehive

Inside a beehive

Bees' entrance

Wooden frames containing honeycomb

Bees and humans

For thousands of years, humans have collected honey and other useful things from bees. At first, early people just stole honey from wild bees' nests, like animals do. But around 6,000 years ago, ancient Egyptians made the first hives for bees to live in, so that it would be easier to collect their honey – and beekeeping was born.

Inside a hive, just as in a wild bees' nest, the bees store their honey in hexagonal cells in the honeycomb. Beekeepers remove the honey by taking out each frame and spinning it in a machine called an extractor. Then they put the frame back in the hive, and the bees fill it with more honey.

Q: What else do we get from bees?

A: As well as honey, beekeepers collect several other useful products from bees:
- **Beeswax** is used to make things like furniture polish, candles and soap.
- **Propolis** is collected by bees from some trees and plant buds. It can be used as a health food.
- **Royal jelly** is a food bees make to feed young queens. It's also used as a health food.

29

Helpful bees and wasps

Besides providing honey, bees and wasps are useful to humans in all sorts of ways. Many wasps help to control crop pest insects, such as caterpillars. And bees help farmers by pollinating their crops. They carry pollen from one flower to another, allowing the plants to make seeds and fruit. Many crops such as apples and alfalfa rely on bees to pollinate them.

Q: How can wasps make ink?

A: Gall wasps are small wasps that lay their eggs in or on plants. The larva releases special saliva that makes the plant grow a round ball, called a gall. The galls contain chemicals that can be used to make black ink. For a long time, most ink was made from wasp galls.

Wasp galls on a leaf

Ichneumon and potter wasps are popular with farmers because they feed on caterpillars and beetle larvae that damage trees and crop plants.

Glossary

Abdomen

One of the three body parts of an insect. All insects have three body parts – a head, a thorax and an abdomen.

Antennae

Feelers found on an insect's head. All insects have two antennae.

Camouflage

The way an animal blends in with its surroundings to escape being noticed by another animal.

Drone

A male bee whose job it is to mate with the queen bee.

Honeycomb

Heagonal-shaped cells made from beeswax. These are often filled with bee larvae or honey.

Honeyguides

The lines found on some flowers which are believed to direct bees to the nectar within the flower.

Larva

A young insect. Larvae can look like a small version of the adult, or they can look completely different.

Mandibles

Mouth organs (jaws) used by insects to seize and bite prey.

Metamorphosis

The striking change some insects go through from larva to adult.

Pheromones

A smell given off by some queen bees and wasps to control the colony.

Pollination

The process by which insects transfer pollen from one flower to another. In doing so, the plant is pollinated and can produce seeds.

Predator

A flesh-eater – an animal that hunts other animals for food.

Prey

An animal that is caught and then eaten by another animal.

Pupa

The stage through which bees and wasps go between being a larva and an adult.

Species

The scientific word for a type of living thing. Animals of the same species can breed together.

Thorax

One of the three body parts of an insect. See abdomen.

Ultraviolet light

A type of light that humans cannot see. However, bees and wasps can see ultraviolet light.

Worker

A female bee whose job it is to take care of the bees' nest and all the bees in it. Worker bees cannot lay eggs.

Index